<u>Mixed Emotionz</u>

<u>by Latoria Gee</u>

<u>My Unique Journey…Fighting Spiritual Warfare…</u>

<u>The Warrior in Me…The Fight from Within…</u>

<u>Disconnected and Misunderstood… Reserved for Restoration…</u>

<u>Shifting to a Better Place! ... Broken to Blessed!</u>

Table of Contents

Foreword

From the very first time I met Latoria "Toi," I knew God had a calling on her life. With a heart like hers, she is constantly on the giving side when it comes to people. God loves such a giving and sincere heart. From the hours of phone conversations, through the ups and downs, I can truly say Latoria has always remained true at heart. Moreover, what many do not know is that she carries a lot of responsibilities. I know from being a believer that the idea is we're supposed to be perfect, showing exemplary amounts of faith for God, but that's why this book Mixed Emotionz is very important. It allows you to see her personal journey, how she has learned and currently understands how to truly trust God. God is all about building on where you are right now. Most of us never really know what a person is going through or dealing with, so we're quick to judge people from what it looks like; you'll never truly know the heart of someone until you learn how to engage with them. Let's learn how to get past the exterior and look at the heart.

Pastor Maurice Bowser
Release Church

From the onset of meeting my God-given, God-ordained, God daughter La'Toria Gee, I knew she was going to be an amazing girl, a powerful young lady, and now a book writer and fully grown woman. She had all the qualities of a high-flying, glamorous celebrity. Even with all of her challenges—every story, every mountain, and every valley—she always had the attitude of a champion, an Eagle that would soar high above every obstacle.

Everything La'Toria set out to do would become a performance—even down to getting dressed: every outfit was complete, with not one piece (including accessories) out of place. Every time we are together is always amazing and filled with life, laughter, and love. She embodies the superstar image with class, charisma, and, most importantly, genuineness. So, when many thought she was mean or angry, it was her mind racing to be excellent, to be great, and to be better.

Today, as I write this foreword to her captivating memoir of her life growing and becoming the woman I see today, I share words that I always hoped—and in many ways knew—I would have the chance to write about her in some amazing way. I often used her and other young ladies and young men to explain that you do not have to settle for less, that you have the power to reach for the stars and obtain God's level best for your life.

Look at you now after every challenge, after every obstacle, you manage to take all of your experiences, whether bad, good, or unexpected, and make them work to positively impact the future. I am so proud of you and not just for this but all your Life's Accomplishments. Be great. Be powerful. Be excellent. Thanks for making your Godfather and so many others proud to be a part of this journey. Tell the story and always keep Christ first in your life.

Love you to life,
Your Godfather
Bishop J Fitzgerald Adams

In every generation, there are voices who are given a rare God-given ability to convey the unexpressed hearts of a generation through their literary work. I wholeheartedly believe La'Toria Gee is one of those voices. I have had the distinct honor of watching La'Toria's journey over the years. She has proven herself amongst colleagues in both professional and faith arenas as an exemplary leader.

Mixed Emotionz is a thought-provoking and candid journey that not only reveals the life of its author but gives a roadmap of hope to each reader. Housed within each chapter, La'Toria shares personal highs, lows, tests, and triumphs. No matter where you may find yourself in life, you are sure to find relevancy in each page that will inspire you to forge ahead in life.

It has been said, "In order to get a sneak peek into a person's drive, take time to listen to the content of their story." Undeniably, Mixed Emotionz reveals the message and mandate of a woman called to be a game changer in the earth. Get ready to dive heart first into this amazing new book.

Torrey Marcel Harper
Itinerant Speaker & Pastor
Habitation Church, NYC

Introduction

Mixed Emotionz came about because I wanted to tell my life's journey and how I survived so many complicated situations, obstacles, and life-threatening circumstances. In this book, I will walk you through many of my personal encounters with God, family, and friends. There are many instances where you will read how I managed to overcome what other people could barely handle. Then, on the other hand, you will learn those times when I allowed my faith to waiver and fail me. I will discuss my health, education, relationships, hobbies, personal interests, and dreams. Let us take a deeper look into my life—the side that no one ever knew about...or maybe what they assumed they knew. I will reveal some of the hidden hurts and painful denunciations. You will read about how I attempted to discover myself in the midst of so much chaos. Get ready for the "uniqueness" of my journey and how I managed to fight through various situations: spiritual warfare, inner thoughts and emotions, being misunderstood, being judged, and conquering through brokenness.

Part 1: Kick Off

Chapter 1: How It All Started

Growing up, life was incredibly challenging and difficult for me. I was born with asthma and had many attacks, which resulted in various hospitalizations. The doctors discovered that I was allergic to shellfish and tree nuts. With so many issues, I found myself lost in a world and could not find my way out of those traumatic situations. Trying to discover who I really was in a dark place was impossible.

So, I was born on December 22, 1985, in an ambulance while my mother was on her way to Germantown Hospital. While the ambulance was driving down Germantown Avenue in the streets of Philadelphia, my mother gave birth to me. It was a rare situation because my mother was not supposed to have a natural birth after having a C-section with my older brother. Well, I was born around 7:30 am in the ambulance and proceeded to the hospital room. At that time, they thought I was a boy because the ambulance EMTs had me wrapped in a baby boy's blanket. It was two long hours that my mother had to wait to see me due to the abnormal delivery. When she was finally able to see me, the head doctor discovered that I was a GIRL! She had the nurses to change me into a soft pink girly blanket.

I am the second born of both of my parents along with being the first-born girl. I have one brother (Pee) and six sisters (Bonnie, Rylee, Tashia, Arianna, Branea, and Brielle). Two sisters are from my mother's side (Tashia and Branea) and four sisters are on my father's side (Bonnie, Rylee, Arianna, and Brielle).

I do not quite remember the things that occurred during my early childhood except attending school, church, and family events. Most of my younger years were centered around religion and the celebration of annual holidays and birthdays. I remember going to amusement parks like Great Adventures, Dorney, Hershey, and Clementon and having Season Passes. I enjoyed spending time with my grandparents, parents, siblings, aunts, uncles, and cousins. I recall parties at Chuck E. Cheese's, where I was petrified of the costumes. I would sit at parties with my eyes closed the entire time and barely enjoyed myself. What I enjoyed most about my juvenile years was hanging out with my family, especially my cousins.

At the age of 12, in 1997, I got saved at a youth retreat at my home church, Fellowship Tabernacle Church under the leadership of the late Bishop R. Taylor, Sr. I was so anxious at a young age to know and learn about this great God. However, I was still suffering on the inside and skeptical if this religious thing was real or not. I remember coming back from our annual youth retreat, and while attending Sunday morning service, my life changed. On this particular Sunday, we had to wear our white tops and black bottoms (skirts) with stockings and black shoes. I was standing at the altar for prayer and felt a heavy wind come over me. My body got so tense, and I began to jump up and down and scream "Jesus!" I even started speaking in an unknown tongue. The Spirit of the Lord came upon me and from that point on I felt such a transformation come over me. I enjoyed singing in the children's choir, attending Vacation Bible School, participating in Sunday School, and any other events conducted by the church.

By the time I was 14 years old, my parents (mother and second-father) started visiting Bethany Baptist Church in New Jersey because we had spontaneously left our home church of over 10 years, Fellowship Tabernacle COGIC. Once again, life had shifted for me without any explanation. Our family decided to join Bethany in 2000; meanwhile, I started attending my God-father's church, Temple of Christian Center, to fill the void that—I believed at the time—I was missing spiritually. While attending two churches during the same period (Bethany in the morning and the Temple in the afternoon), I was able to unite with my sisters Bonnie, Rylee, and Arianna.

Because of the bond that my sisters and I had formed, I figured it was time to reach out to my biological father, Garrett. I contacted my father but did not receive the response I wanted. I left it alone; I almost gave up because I felt like I should not be the one initiating a relationship with a man whose whole family had denied me since birth. I waited two years: it was then 2002. This time I was adamant about a relationship with my father because there were some unanswered questions. The void I was feeling was due to the lack of support, concern, and security that I never had received from my father. Most of my life, I felt rejected and disappointed by the men I was surrounded by rather than protected and covered. Even though I had a stepfather who was there for me and my siblings, there was nothing like the feeling of my biological father being a part of my life.

My second-father, Bradford, was a family man and very supportive of me, my brother Pee, and my sister Tashia. He ensured that we were active in sports, church, and community events. At times, he and my mother were very strict due to our religious (Christian) beliefs. Many times, my siblings and I were not allowed to participate in school functions, such as Halloween parties, school dances, and afterschool events. Now that I am older, I understand because they groomed me to have a better understanding and perspective of adhering to the religious doctrines/standards. For example, most times after a school dance, there was a fight or some conflict that occurred with my school associates, which required the police to be involved. So, I do appreciate my parents for saying "No" at times. Although I missed the opportunity to socialize with many fellow classmates outside of school, I was able to obtain a uniqueness about myself.

I remember growing up and before we left the house, my mother and my stepfather would read bible scriptures with us and put holy oil on our foreheads. I honestly am grateful for the spiritual foundation because it protected us from many dangers, neighborhood violence, and any unwanted attacks. For instance, when we lived on Sterling Street in Philadelphia, Pennsylvania, I remember that our next-door neighbors were drug dealers. This one particular time, Kareem and Johnny got into a verbal altercation, and later on that evening, the opponent came back around the block and shot up their house. There were such loud gunshot triggers; all I could hear was the glass shattering at our neighbor's, windows along with our front door. I recall lying on the wooden floor in our dining room with my hands over my ears, thinking to myself, "When will this ever end?" Mind you, this was not the first nor the last time a shooting occurred on our block/neighborhood. So that situation takes me back to my parents covering us spiritually to ensure we were safe.

At the age of 16, my father and I began our journey to rekindle a relationship that many family members did not believe would ever reemerge. From that point forward, we bonded and built a relationship that was inseparable. I was so excited about spending time at my father's house with him and my sisters. I would sleep over at my father's house during the weekends. I remember going to the nail salon to get our nails done, ordering pizza from Nick's, taking pictures at the Cheltenham Mall, and shopping at Rainbow for clothes. Although my father worked many hours during the course of the week, that did not stop him from spending time with his children when he could. I would look forward to going over there so my sisters and I could get on the "Loop Party Line." We used that to communicate with our church friends who were long distance and to meet new boys (lol).

On Sunday mornings, my dad would drive us to his church, Mt. Moriah Pentecostal Church (although he did not attend consecutively…hahaha). We were dropped off at church just in time for Sunday School, which I thought was very boring but necessary. Most weekends I felt like we were tortured to sit in a church with a bunch of older people singing hymns and testifying about their week. I would sit in Mt. Moriah Pentecostal Church and count down the time until we could leave so that we could catch the L bus, orange line, and 206 New Jersey transit just to get to the Temple of Love. We would have to leave Mt. Moriah by 1:35pm just to get to the Temple by 4:00pm. I was now fully active at the Temple of Love Christian Center under the leadership of my Godfather Fitzgerald, where I ushered, sang on the choir/praise team, and was the pastor's adjutant.

I started dating my boyfriend, Alex, at the time. I found myself buying out our relationship. I would use my entire paycheck to buy him clothes, sneakers, and food. However, in return all he wanted was sex from me. Because I was looking for something I could not identify at that time, I found myself being abused financially and once again emotionally. I moved out and lived with him after an altercation at my parents' home. After being together for almost 2 years, I discovered that he had cheated on me and had a baby on the way. I broke up with him, and once again I was covering up reality. I moved back to my parents' house—something I did not want to do since I made a vow to myself that once I moved out, I was never to return.

In 2003, at the age of 18, I was licensed as a Junior Evangelist, under the leadership of my Godfather Fitzgerald. I remembered crying in prayer the night before because I knew God had called me for this assignment and I did not want to let Him down. I prayed that God's will be done in my life and that He would free me from any emotional and broken distress. I refused to minister to people out of my emotions because that was one thing I disliked about preachers. I felt like it was not the time to throw off my life obstacles or experiences in the pulpit. Preaching was a time to heal, deliver, and encourage others through the Word of God. However, I found myself still ministering yet broken and did not know how I was going to be liberated. I travelled from Norristown to Philadelphia to Camden, New Jersey, with my sisters Rylee and Bonnie weekly. However, I felt like I was still missing something essential in my life.

I preached my initial sermon: Matthew 5:44 "Love Your Enemies," and that is when I determined to love others despite the damage they had caused me. After receiving prophesy after prophesy about how gifted and anointed I was, it was in that moment I knew God had truly ordained me for the rest of my life. I preached about loving ourselves, along with those who have hurt us. I explained how important it is to have a forgiving heart and to be free from the bondage of how others may have felt about us or treated us. I also expounded on how it was and still is important to do unto others how we expect them to handle us. Blessing others with our positive energy despite their negativity towards us is crucial—being courteous and helpful no matter if our enemies hate us. Show them that you love them just as Christ loves us. I told the church how it was important to pray for our adversaries so that we can live with peace within ourselves. We cannot change how people treat us, but we have the power to dictate how we respond to others.

I knew I was called to the ministry because of my gift of discernment and dreams. When I first started dreaming, it scared me because God would show me things in dreams prior to them occurring. It felt like a warning/sign before the actual event occurred. When I had dreams, I would wake up in the middle of the night with my heart beating fast and breathing heavily. I remember telling my mother about dreaming of two black dogs chasing me in an alley and one of them bit me. My mother said, "You have to pray after your dreams and ask God to reveal to you what He is trying to tell you." The next day I went to work and discovered that my two supervisors were trying to give me corrective action for an incident they had assumed I was a part of. I was saddened because they were determined to terminate me; they had created a plan for me to meet with them weekly. Long story short, I refused to sign and met with Human Resources to get a better understanding of what the write-up was about. All in all, their plan was not rendered because the situation was not precise. I mentioned that dream to explain how God warns me about good and bad situations in my dreams. The dreams are so intense at times that I cannot even go back to sleep. I appreciate the fact that I can discuss my dreams with my mother, and she can interpret them at times or guide me in how I should move forward.

Later in 2003, I moved out again with my second boyfriend, but that only lasted about two months. So, I moved back home.

Meanwhile, I was still flopping among church concerts, events, and services because I sang with many local gospel groups. I reconnected with Blaine who has been a great friend in my life. Of course, we had to deal with the rumors of us dating, but we ignored them and remained genuinely friends. Blaine and I would sing together and harmonize to songs, especially gospel and R&B soul. One thing I appreciate about Blaine was that he taught me how to drive a vehicle. I was scared about driving, but he remained calm and patient with me. Blaine made so many sacrifices after concerts to take me home to Norristown or Philadelphia because he lived in Pennsauken, New Jersey. During those moments, we shared our experiences and desires with each other. I recall driving around looking at mansions in Cherry Hill, New Jersey; we would say to each other, "One day, we will have a house like this." I value our friendship even today as we collaborate about singing, church, family, and life in general. To this day, I visit Blaine's home, or he comes to mine, so that we can just chat and catchup with each other.

Even though I was a member of Bethany, I was still wandering in and out of churches. To be honest, I was very unstable and unbalanced. I got tired of shouting and being emotionalized by church leaders; I was ready for substance, teaching, and structure. I decided to rejoin Bethany in 2005, at the age of 20-years-old. I became an active member and volunteered in several ministries: choir, angel food bank, and wherever I felt I was needed. I felt good about my life; I reapplied to Community College of Philadelphia for my Associate's Degree in Business. Blaine and I joined the choir because one day as we were once again harmonizing while walking down the walkway, Winston (who is also a friend of mine) turned around and said, "Y'all should join the choir."

I was finally at a point in my life when and where I felt like I was mature enough to move out on my own. I went to work at Rites Institution of America, and the next day, I searched online for some apartments while my coworkers helped me. I found nothing, still no hope. During that week, I picked up the Philadelphia Inquirer and saw an apartment available in Wynnefield, Pennsylvania.

I was eager for change and something different in my life, so I purchased *Healed Without Scars* by Bishop Evans. Reading the book helped me control my emotions until I moved months later. What helped me, particularly, was "Chapter 3: The Causes of Our Pain" (pp.39-48). In that chapter, Bishop Evans discusses emotional scars and how they are constant reminders that we are suffering from past hurts. He mentions that we need to learn how to recognize the many obstacles and trials that we have faced and respond to them by our faith. Tests typically reveal our character while trials uncover the truth and fakeness around us. When I read the part that "Jesus wants to carry the weight of my experience," I had a different revelation of why Jesus died on the cross and was wounded for me.

I realized that I had to endure that part of the process in order for me to be "healed without scars."

There is nothing like not knowing why you have to face such obstacles in life until you really have an encounter with God. I can honestly say that I do not know how I managed to get through the process, but I was able to conquer it. Until then, people were calling me "mean-spirited," but, in all actuality, I was broken on the inside and had no way of living through life challenges. I had to literally face people and respect them although they disrespected, mistreated, and abused me.

Chapter 2: Cultivation Through Education

I remember attending Penny Packer Elementary School with my brother and cousins. I recollect one parent and teacher service day when the teacher called me by the incorrect name; my mother turned and said "Letora" is not her name—it is "Latoria."

Mrs. Jonez, who was my teacher at the time, looked at me and said, "Do not ever allow anyone to call you by the wrong name."

I looked up at her with such embarrassment and stated, "Yes, ma'am, I totally understand."

During that time, we lived in the high-rise apartments on Clearview Street in Philadelphia, Pennsylvania. The teacher was so proud of the fact that I was quiet yet intelligent. She mentioned to my mother that she believed the class was not appropriate for me. Mrs. Jonez put in a recommendation letter for me to be skipped to the next grade. I remember sitting at this long round table with a bunch of committee board members, along with my mother who was a single parent. Everyone agreed that I was too advanced for 1st grade and decided to skip me to 2nd grade.

We moved to another area of Philadelphia (West Oak Lane), and I switched schools. I recall walking to Rowan Elementary school in a snow blizzard wearing my pink snowsuit. The snow was so high (up to our hips), but we still had to walk to school. One day it was so cold, we complained the entire walk to school; however, we made it safely. I remember always walking many blocks to attend school, but it was fun because I was able to spend time with my friends and family. My time at that school was short lived because we moved to Norristown, Pennsylvania, and I started attending Marshall Street Elementary School. Attending a new school in a predominately white neighborhood, I began to experience a diverse group of students.

I was teased by fellow classmates because my menstrual cycle came on for the first time at school. I remember standing up in class and there was blood on my tan seat. I was so embarrassed, nervous, and afraid because I did not know what to do. I told my teacher Mrs. Cater, and she allowed me to change my clothes and clean off the seat. After that occurred, I asked to go to the nurse's office so that I could go home early. I was able to have my mother pick me up from school. My mother explained to me what was happening with my body. We had a mother-daughter talk, and she informed me about the importance of tracking my cycle in a hand calendar and showed me how to use pads and maintain clean hygiene.

While attending Marshall Street, I was able to join the choir. I really did not have any friends because I was the new girl from Philadelphia "who thought she was better than everyone else." My fellow classmates started teasing me and stated that I smelled like "Raid roach spray and pee." I used to cry walking home because I could not believe that students my age were so cruel. I knew I did not smell that way because my mom made sure we always had a spotless house and clean hygiene. The good thing about attending Marshall Street was that I was able to check on my little sister Tashia and peek in her classroom when I walked down the hallway. I graduated from Marshall Street and finally moved on to middle school.

Stewart Middle School was where I finally started defending myself. I remember still being teased and laughed at about the clothes I wore and how the other kids said that I "smelled like pee." One day I was sitting in class, and this one girl put her index finger up and acted like she was spraying and held her nose. I finally asked her to stop, and she said she was going to beat me up after school. So, the rule was if you went home first after school, then the school district was no longer responsible if you got into some sort of trouble/fight. Well, I told her to meet me after school at my house. To my surprise, Blake showed up at my house with her friend Avery because she was serious about fighting me. I remember fighting Blake in my front yard while her friend stood there watching. When I finished whooping Blake's butt, I asked her friend if she wanted to get beat up, too. I recall my brother coming outside and asking what was going on, and I told him that I had just beat Blake up for teasing me. He told Blake and Avery to leave and informed me to go into the house. Once my mother got home from work, I explained to her what had happened. She said, "Good," but I could tell she was disappointed in my actions.

Well, it did not stop there... A year later, I was in seventh grade and remember being teased by Cordell. He slapped me with an open hand while walking in the hall. Rumor got around, and my brother found out. While walking home from school, I saw a crowd of young people in the alleyway between Hamilton Street and

Marshall Street. I made my way through the crowd and discovered that it was my brother and Cordell fighting because he had slapped me. Of course, my brother was winning the fight. I decided to jump in and started kicking Cordell with my sneakers while he was still on the ground.

Here we go to eighth grade, the last year of middle… I thought the teasing would eventually stop. I was sitting in the auditorium, and there was so much noise because we had to wait indoors to report to class due to the rain. Well, Makayla turned around and told me stop screaming in her ear. I looked at her and rolled my eyes and said, "Little girl, I was not even saying anything."

Makayla kept talking to her friend and seconds later, what did she do? Turned around and screamed at me, "B****, didn't I tell you to stop yelling in my ear?" Makayla then lifted her arm, balled up her fist, and proceeded to charge at me. I remember blocking her hit and fighting her. I slipped on the water due to the wet floors, but when I finished with her butt, the teachers were pulling me off of her. As a result of fighting, Makayla and I were both reprimanded with in-school suspension (ISS). We were sitting in the ISS room, and I turned around and told her that I was going to whoop her a** after school again, "Watch me." Due to Makayla and I's fighting, they let us out at two different times. Of course, once that afternoon

2:45 bell rang, I went looking for her after school, but Makayla was nowhere to be found.

I finally let that situation pass and began to focus on the good things, such as enjoying school and learning more in my education. At Stewart, I remember Math, Social Studies, Music, English, and Science. I remember the Science fairs and asking my parents for money to pay for books. My favorite time was Homeroom when I developed friendships with Daniel, Patrice, India, James, and Gracey. We had our school dance that year, and I remember begging my parents to allow me to attend the dance. At first, they were reluctant due to our religious beliefs. My mother finally gave in and allowed me to attend the school dance. Days and weeks went by, and I formed great relationships with two teachers who believed in me: Mrs. Garvey and Mr. Botley. Those two teachers really impacted my life and encouraged me to follow every dream and desire I chased after. I remember being a part of field hockey, choir, lacrosse, and track. I really enjoyed our yearly field days. We would have to wear certain colors for each group and compete for a prize which was typically a pizza party. I graduated from Stewart on the honor roll with perfect attendance. One fond memory I have from Middle School was in Music class when Mr. Wright would have us playing the triangles and singing to the music he played through the cassette player. One thing I do regret is not learning how to read music because I really looked forward to that class along with singing on the choir.

In 2003, I graduated from high school and received a scholarship for the Most Successful in my class. I received that award because in 9th grade I got into some trouble (which was my fault), was fighting, got locked up and, as a result, was in the process of being expelled. I remember the day I went back to Stewart Middle School and approached one of my old friends....

I got off the bus, and all I could hear was the noise of instigators saying, "Beat her *tail!*" (Well, they were actually cursing.) When I saw Destiny (my old friend) walking to the corner of Marshall Street and Forest Avenue, I could feel my heart beating so fast. I was not scared but anxious about the fight I was about to get into. As we approached each other, I could feel my fist balling up and eventually going across her face. As we fought, I picked Destiny up and dropped her to the ground; we both wound up on the pavement. I managed to get back up and started kicking her with my foot. I felt myself being grabbed by two sets of strong, heavy hands: Mr. Thompson (teacher) and Mr. Greeze (Assistant Principal). Next thing I knew, the cops were handcuffing me into the back of the cop car. I was processed as a minor and issued a $1,000 fine for disrupting the peace. I recall sitting in a dark police station thinking, "What did I get myself into?" My parents finally came to pick me up, and they were not happy. I had to attend juvenile court, pay the fine issued by the judge, and participate in community service. Once the fine was paid off, my case was dismissed.

As a result of the fight, I was in the process of suspension, pending an expelling from Norristown Area High School. However, there were teachers and other faculty members who were advocating for me to stay at the High School. I was able to pay my fine weekly from my paychecks (working at my aunt's boarding home) but received in-house school suspension. During that suspension, I was favored; I was afforded the opportunity to work in the school office and assist the Secretary to the Principal, along with the Librarian with organizing books in the library. I received the Perfect Attendance Award as well because my mother made us go to school every day. We could not miss school even if we were near death's door (hahahahaha).

In 2004, I started attending Community College of Philadelphia. I was in school for Business and always wanted to launch my own corporation. I was not sure at that time, but I wanted to do something on my own. However, because of my finances, I was not able to finish school. I started working at Party City to save up money and paid for one class at a time. I was in/out of taking courses due to various reasons. I was finally able to apply for financial aid and obtain some sort of monetary resource. Although it took me some time, I finished school and graduated in May 2014 with my Associate's Degree in Business. Community College of Philadelphia was necessary for me because I learned so many skills (computer, leadership, communication, time management, and critical thinking/problem solving) from the various courses I had to take. I met so many people from diverse backgrounds, as well, and developed interpersonal relationships.

In August 2014, I registered at Strayer University and began to take intense courses. I applied for financial aid again and was eligible for funding towards my curricula. I attended school full-time while working full-time as a Day Program Coordinator of two vocational day programs and one supported employment program. It was particularly challenging, but I pushed forward through my circumstances because I knew the ending was going to be greater. During my time at Strayer, I received many awards for my academic achievements. I was so proud of myself and how determined I was to make a difference in my life. Many days, I did not want to attend class on campus, but I pressed through the hurdles and kept moving. I remember the late nights and early mornings of studying. I declined many events (parties, social gatherings, singing engagements, etc.) because school and work were both my priorities. I obtained my Bachelor's Degree in May 2017 in Business Administration with a 3.89 GPA. I can remember hearing my name as I walked across the stage of the stadium in Washington, D.C.

filled with thousands of people. To hear "Latoria Denise Gee; Summa cum Laude" was such a proud moment for me, especially while my family and friends shouted my name.

I decided to keep going and go for my graduate degree. In August 2017, I was accepted to Wilmington University as a full-time student. While still working full-time, I was able to maintain a 4.0 GPA., writing a thesis, taking weekly quizzes, participating in daily discussions, and drafting short papers. Looking back, I do not know how I was able to manage such great tasks and graduate in less than two years. It was definitely a struggle to say the least. However, I did not let the oppositions stop me from maintaining my curriculum goals. Even when I felt defeated, I prayed to God, cried, and reassured myself that it was all worth the fight. I thank God for my two friends Rodney and Yah because we were able to reassure one another that we were going to excel and soar through the program. In January 2019, I obtained my Master's Degree in Human Resource Management. It was nothing but the "Grace of God." I felt so accomplished: I finally achieved another one of my greatest goals.

Chapter 3: Radical Relationships

Where do I begin? Well... I started dating at the age of 15-years-old. Yeah, I know that is young, but that is what I decided to do. I was still in high school and, to be exact, in the eleventh grade. I attended Norristown Area High School, where and when I met my first male friend. We met by locking eyes while walking down the cream-colored hallways filled with orange lockers. Zayden asked me for my number, and we exchanged words. Later that evening around 7:00pm, Zayden called me on my prepaid phone (a black, flip Motorola). We only talked for about ten minutes because I did not want to use up my prepaid time. Months went by, and we got to know each other a little more. I learned that Zayden liked basketball and enjoyed spending time with his family. We would meet at the East Side Library and do schoolwork, as well. However, the friendship did not last long because he was graduating and wanted to part ways.

I remember sitting in service at 16-years-old and watching this light-skinned, tall young man walk in with a crowd of people. The church I was attending was having afternoon service. As the young man got closer to me, we smiled at each other and proceeded to enjoy the worship service. I recall standing outside the church with my sisters Rylee and Bonnie on Federal Street in Camden after service. While discussing the service, we were interrupted by another young man named Bryan. Bryan began to express his brethren's interest in me and wanted to know if I had a boyfriend at the time.

I said, "No, but if your brother wants to talk to me or if he has any questions, then he can come to me!"

Bryan said, "Wow, you do not play, I see."

He walked away, and minutes later I turned around to see the young man walking out of the double glass doors. He walked up to me and my sisters and introduced himself as Alex. He asked if I was in a relationship, and I said "No." We then exchanged numbers and went about our ways.

Anyone who knows me knows that I am not the pursuer, so I did not call Alex that night nor the next day. I waited for Alex to call me to prove that he was interested in me. Days went by, then he finally called me. We talked about the church service and how we looked forward to our churches fellowshipping again. Alex and I began to share information about our pasts and our goals for the future. We even talked about our favorite foods, colors, our middle names, etc. As time went on, we became closer and started to build a true, genuine friendship. Our hangout spot was the "Philadelphia Gallery." We would go there to eat, shop, take pictures, and just enjoy each other. I remember one time we decided to take pictures at "Picture People" and wanted to match so badly that we wore blue shirts, denim bottoms, and blue sneakers/shoes. We did so much together, like travel on the train from Pennsylvania to New Jersey to New York.

Months went by, and we decided to make it an official relationship. It was like the perfect relationship until one day I received a phone call while I was working at Party City. I answered the phone and was given disturbing news by one of Alex's family members that he was cheating on me with several females. I was so devastated that I had to clock out for a break. I remember hanging up the phone with the family member to call Alex. Of course, he did not answer, so I left him a message on his phone and told him that I was done: "I hope the grass is greener on the other side." Alex finally called me back a few days later to try to explain that it was not that deep and that I did not need to listen to his family because they were jealous of our relationship. We talked about what had happened days prior. I still had some reluctance, so I decided to end the relationship to avoid being hurt. I am glad that I decided to follow my heart because later that year Alex got another girl pregnant.

Did I think that was enough to stay single? Well, no... I allowed another young man to pursue me months later. I remember sitting at the "Temple"; the church was on the corner of 36th and

Merriel Avenue in Camden, New Jersey. When I walked in, the church was crowded with people due to a musical. I could hear this vibrant voice in the microphone singing. There was such a heavy anointing in his voice that I knew he was destined to be great. Once again after service, we had a conversation, and he told me his name was Dawson and gave me his number written in pencil on a white receipt from the APlus gas station. I waited a week and finally called him. We decided to go to a diner one Saturday afternoon. He picked me up from my parents' house in Norristown around 3:05pm and drove me back to New Jersey to the Audubon Diner. I ordered a bacon cheeseburger with lettuce, tomato, and ketchup with a side of fries. We talked about his goals to travel and my desire to sing background for someone famous one day. We checked out and headed to church because he had to play the bass for a dedication service. Months went by, and then he wanted to break up with me. I was so shocked that I wanted to jump out of the car. Reality truly hit me, and I realized—after I had moved in with him—that we were not meant to be with one another. There was a lot of dishonesty and disconnect between the two of us. I realized that we had many differences and were both living life in two separate directions.

As years went by, I decided to stay single but dated, of course. However, I always seemed to attract men who were sneaky, leaching, lying, or had many children. I made a vow to myself that I would not date anyone with children, especially adolescents. Do not get me wrong, I love children and hold them dear to my heart, but I had my mind made up that I would not put myself in a convoluted situation with another man.

I also attracted men who were already in serious relationships or married. I would typically get inboxes on Myspace, Twitter, Facebook Messenger, or Instagram (direct messages). It was very frustrating for me because I was never one to date anyone who was already in a committed relationship. I believe it shows the utmost disrespect to the other female—or male. Yes, I said "male" because I attracted bisexual men, as well. I never went to the next level with these men because I knew what the consequences would be if I were to disrupt someone else's relationship. I even had guys lie to my face and tell me that they were single, but when I scrolled onto their social media accounts, they were posting their significant other. One thing I did not ever tolerate was disrespect or insulting my intelligence.

In 2009, I met my best friend Yah who has been a blessing to me. He has supported me in so many areas of my life. Yah encouraged me to pursue my education when I felt there was no need to keep going. He has inspired me to perceive life outside of church. If it were not for Yah, I would probably still be roaming around in and out of concerts and churches. I remember when I first met Yah at my previous job in the kitchenette area. We had talked for a bit but not long due to him being in the annual training. A year went by, and then I saw Yah in one of the retraining classes; I waved at him while he was sitting in the training room. Being smart, he turned around as if I was not speaking to him. Once again, he came into the kitchenette area, and this time we exchanged numbers and personal information. That evening we became Facebook friends, and the rest has been history. Yah has had my back with everything, and I mean everything—down to paying my bills, celebrating milestones, and supporting my goals. Of course, we fuss at each other here and there, but we have learned to respect each other's viewpoints. Yah has shown me how a man should treat me and take care of me. I appreciate all the sacrifices he has made for the past twelve years to ensure that I was okay. Yah and I share religious standpoints and private information, along with reassuring one another that we have each other. I remember this one particular time when we went to Vegas for the first time. We had such a great experience; we engaged in so many attractions: The Grand Canyon, museums, comedy shows, etc. We honestly had a blast, and I really enjoy the bond we have created. Yah and I have so many fond memories that I could write another book about our friendship.

From the age of 18-years-old to present, I have dated men, but none of them attracted me in such a way that I would move forward into an intense relationship. However, there are many things I tend to look for in a man:

- ✓ Consistency: He should not flip flop back and forth in his feelings toward me. I am always expecting the man to maintain his attitude and behavior.
- ✓ Verbal communication: He should tell me what he wants and what his expectations are from me. I cannot read anyone's mind and do not desire to do so either.
- ✓ Stability: He should be steady, unchangeable, and a man who has a good handle on his life, goals, and emotions.
- ✓ Support: I want my man to be by my side and push me into greatness and assist me as needed with any goals or desires.
- ✓ Love: He should be intimate and affectionate with me—no matter what my past looks like.
- ✓ Fears God: I want a man who has a relationship with God and understands the importance of adhering to the Bible and God's commands.
- ✓ Trust: Without trust, we cannot move in a unified commitment. Whenever a man or woman has trust concerns, they can cause conflict within a relationship.
- ✓ Respect: This refers to the way I am treated or thought of through a man's eyes: how polite, genuine, caring, and kind the man is concerning me.

All in all, I expect to be treated and handled with the utmost value and regard. I will never lower my standards for another man so that he could love me unconditionally. I will continue to stay true to myself and follow God's plan for a relationship. I do not plan on ever being the pursuer in a relationship because I never have done so. I bring many qualities and worth into a bond so that I would continue to pull my weight and do my part to please my man/husband.

It is important to build a friendship and learn as much about the other person prior to moving forward into a serious relationship. I tell you this: when you become friends, you obtain so much knowledge,about the other person. You can build a foundation of love and sturdiness. It would be difficult for anyone to try and break or destroy what the two have worked so hard to build.

Part 2: Staying the Course

Chapter 4: Am I Being Catfished?

In August 2014, one of my direct employees (Jessa) approached me about her brother Hymed's liking me. I did not entertain her at first because I had never seen her brother. Jessa claimed that he had seen me singing at a concert. After about a month or so, she came back to me and stated that her brother was interested in me. I said, "Okay," and she gave me his number. She came to work and asked why I did not contact her brother (Hymed). I said, "Because I was busy."

Later that evening, I received a text from a number that I believed was the brother at that time. We exchanged some talk in conversation. Months went by, and we finally scheduled to meet each other. I went to the location (Bahama Breeze), but he never showed up. I found that to be very odd because he seemed so interested in meeting me. The next day, I received a text that he had gotten sick that night. As the year came to an end, this guy (Hymed) and I had never met, nor had we ever seen each other. In 2015, meeting locations were scheduled but fell through. I eventually gave up. I knew there was something very strange about this situation, but I was naïve and ignored the warning signs.

I started receiving flowers at my job from the floral shop and notes on the front door of my house. I then asked the sister (Jessa) what was up with her brother (Hymed) and who had given him my address. I knew my direct employee (Jessa) had my address because a few of the workers had met at my house for an event to support one of our co-workers the previous year. Well, she denied giving him my address and acted clueless about the flowers.

In May 2015, Mother's Day to be exact, I received a call from my direct employee (Jessa) that her brother (Hymed) was in a tragic accident on Route 295 in Bordentown, New Jersey. I immediately went into prayer and asked God to protect and heal the brother. She called me back and said he was in ICU in Capital Heart Medical–Hope City. I told her that I would come, but she said "No," not at the time. Meanwhile, I had never seen this brother (Hymed) other than alleged pics on his Instagram and had only talked to him over the phone a few times.

Well, over months of Hymed being in and out of the hospital, my direct employee (Jessa) started clinging to me. In between all this, her father had allegedly died. I was able to collect over $750 from my staff to support her and her family. We arranged to attend the funeral, but Jessa lied about the location. It was to the point that a few of the co-workers had attended the funeral of this unknown man. We convened at work the next Monday and concluded that something was not right with this young lady. Jessa started calling me her mentor, big sis, and advisor; eventually, I did not entertain her because I knew she was up to something.

Finally, I started investigating as I typically would do when things do not seem right. Therefore, I decided to contact the floral shop because flowers were sent to my job for the third time. The "Love Me Floral Shop" attendant informed me that it was my direct employee (Jessa), and she had seemed nervous when she placed an order at their shop. The floral shop attendant also stated that Jessa was very demanding about the time that she needed the flowers sent to my job. That was crazy because Jessa had asked if she could go home that day because she had an emergency with her brother. Later that week, I could not sleep so I went on Instagram and searched all the friends on the alleged brother Hymed's page and stumbled upon a familiar picture. This photo was one of the ones that was sent to my phone portraying to be the brother. I direct messaged the person who was being impersonated and informed him that someone was stealing his pictures. We became Instagram friends, and he was appreciative that I had informed him. Within minutes, I started getting all these phone calls from a blocked number. I did not answer and decided to block my employee Jessa and the alleged brother Hymed's numbers. Furthermore, this person started calling my house number, and it showed up on the caller ID as my direct employee Jessa's number. I knew at that point she was catfishing me.

Jessa came to work the next day and started acting like she was vomiting so that she could get my attention. I ignored her and did not feed into her attention-seeking behaviors. I noticed that she started waiting for me in the lobby after work, so I informed Human Resources and wrote a statement to protect myself and my position. It was so intense that I called her later that week and told her that I would beat her tail (well…a few curse words are what I told her) if she did not leave me alone and stop harassing me. I said some other things, and she eventually understood what I was saying to her. Jessa went on to her next victim and got terminated for her actions.

All in all, I was upset and extremely disappointed that I had allowed someone to catfish me into a situation. I learned that I cannot be naïve and nonchalant to people and circumstances. I realized that I need to follow the voice of God and discern what is real or not.

Chapter 5: The Complex Part to Complete Healing

In 2012, both my maternal and two paternal grandmothers became ill. I found myself juggling school, work, and my personal life while helping to care for my grandmothers. All three were in and out of hospitals and rehabs for over a year with life-threatening illnesses. I prayed, fasted, and believed God for complete and total healing; however, in 2013, my maternal grandmother became very ill. I doubted God once again because He was not doing what I thought He had promised me—and that was healing for my grandmother.

Well, on November 1st, life took the best of me…My grandmother died, and I felt so shattered. I could not understand what had happened: How and why my grandmother? I found myself driving to the cemetery and to her house because I just could not believe she was gone. My grandmother was no longer here. The one who made my clothes, inspired me to read the Bible, showed me how to bake, and talked to me about bettering my future was never going to talk to me again. As time went on, I was able to cope with the fact that she was not coming back. However, I still have moments when I miss her dearly.

It is unfortunate that years later on July 17, 2019, I had to relive losing my paternal grandmother. My Nana who always took me shopping, cooked dinners, loved eating, and spent hours on the phone gossiping about family members was no longer here. I had to regroup and recoup with yet another loss. I definitely have many moments when I miss talking to her on the phone and conversing about her career path. When she passed it was like another hole was ripped from my chest. I say that because I was with her during her illnesses and never imagined that she would not be here with me to share fond memories.

From 2014 to present, I have supported family members who are in and out of hospitals, rehabs, and nursing homes. I have become everyone's primary person of support for medical illnesses. I visit family, friends, and co-workers during their crises. I advocate for patients who are terminally ill, transitioning in/out of facilities or just needed overall support. I exhibit these skills by asking doctors/nurses questions, talking to the patients to assist them in understanding their diagnoses, and corresponding with their family members. It is easy for me to do what I am doing because I love helping, praying, supporting, and encouraging others. I am the one who would randomly visits sick people and takes them cards and/or just sit with them and watch television. I advocate for people like my grandmothers, grandfather, great-aunts, uncles, friends, my friend's parents, and co-workers.

However, things did not become severely complex until it became personal for me. In March 2017, I passed out on the plane on my way to Las Vegas, Nevada. I thought it was due to being dehydrated and the lack of eating that morning. It was not until I passed out and fainted in June 2017, weeks before graduating from Strayer University, that I decided to get checked at Genesis Hospital. The ER doctor told me nothing was wrong and sent me home. However, I knew that something was wrong with my body. I scheduled an appointment with my primary doctor who ordered bloodwork and additional testing and learned that I had Grave's disease (hyperactive thyroid). I was devastated because during that visit, my heart rate was over 200. The doctor checked my heart again and was concerned that I had a heart murmur. With tears in my eyes, I prayed and trusted God for healing. In August 2017, to rule out a heart murmur, I had to wear a heart monitor for five days. The doctor then ordered/scheduled an ultrasound of my heart, throat, and stomach. The tests came back negative for a heart murmur and nothing irregular with my thyroid. I was prescribed medications for my thyroid and increased heart rate. I prayed over those medications and declared that I was healed.

In April 2018, life really began to become even more complex. I requested Family Medical Leave from my job because of anxiety, my thyroid, and a stress disorder. I literally felt my head spinning some days while I was at work. I sought much needed help due to the stress and anxiety I was facing at that time. It was to the point that I was shaking and trembling when I thought about how my life was operating. I became so overwhelmed with the unnecessary attacks I was dealing with that I decided to seek a professional counselor for assistance. I scheduled sessions for two times a week. Session after session, I felt myself falling into a deeper depression; I would sit in the session and express my deeper, inner feelings. I could not grasp nor understood why I was a target everywhere in my life. I felt like I was in a hole—like a groundhog who could not see its own shadow. I did not know if I was coming or going.

I recall this one particular session when I literally cried the entire time. While tears were falling down my face, Dr. Hechet said, "Tori, you have to free yourself from being accountable for everyone else's decisions in life." I found myself living a life to accommodate everyone else but me. At that moment, I knew it was time for me to live for me, but I was not ready for that change to take place yet.

Time went on... Counseling sessions still were active; however, I was still in a dark place. It was to the point that I was laying in the bed all day under the covers. Most times, I was not even eating nor talking to anyone. I separated myself from family members and friends: I just wanted to be alone. The doctor wanted to diagnose me with depression and anxiety and give me medications to take me out of the mental state I was in at the time. I refused to allow any medical provider to diagnose me with pills or medicate me. Instead, I stopped attending the sessions and focused on the next task that was grasping my attention, which was my father.

Amid all the mental health crises, I still continued to sing and serve at many ministries and churches. At this one particular time in June 2018, I attended a concert. I did not want to be there, but my sister Bonnie begged me to go sing with my Godfather, Bishop Fitzgerald's choir. The choir sang "We Offer Praise," and after we finished ministering, I sat down on the second row. As I sat in a reserved mood for the remainder of the service, the speaker finally got up. She was a tall, thick, brown lady with a short bob wearing a long purple robe with rhinestones around the collar. While in the service, unengaged and watching everyone jump around, yell, and scream like circus animals, I sat in such disconnect. I paid attention to how this preacher (Dr. Charmaine Patkinson) ministered and prophesied over various people's lives. Annoyed with the circus that was going on around me, I was finally ready to go. However, my parents taught my siblings and I to stay at events, venues, or services until the end. I really did not care what was imparted into me at that time; I was ready to go (lol).

As I was getting ready to grab my coat, Dr. Patkinson looked at me and said, "Do you like me?"

My response was, "Yes," yet I was annoyed even more.

Dr. Patkinson looked over at my Godfather, Bishop Fitzgerald, and asked for permission to speak (prophesy over my life). My Godfather shook his head "yes." Dr. Patkinson looked at me and said, "This next season in your life is going to be such a life-changing experience…" She proceeded to say, "I am going to give you the strength that I needed to get through what I had experienced." She then blew her breath into my mouth (at which I instantly became infuriated because I have issues with people touching me as well as being in my personal space). As she continued to speak over my life, all I could remember her saying was, "This next season you are about to encounter, you are going to need much strength."

Not knowing that then I actually needed it because that is what got me through some of the toughest times in my life. At first, I am going to be honest, I thought Dr. Patkinson had put a curse on my life, and I am going to tell you why... Those next few months were nothing but pure hell. Another reason why her speaking over my life did not sit well with me at the time is because typically it was really rare when someone prophesied to me. I would say 95% of the time when someone speaks into my life, they are accurate. It amazes me that almost three years later, I can remember Dr. Patkinson's exact words, what happened during the service, the month, and where I was sitting. God is so strategic in how He works, and He never ceases to amaze me.

Well let me proceed... While out on FMLA, my father became severely ill. He faced many medical challenges and agreed to surgery. However, during the surgery I was not expecting the doctor to inform me that my father had some sort of cancer. Holding strong to my faith and believing God, I looked at the doctor and said, "Okay." Weeks went by, and the doctor informed my father, while I was visiting him, that he had Stage Four Colon Adenocarcinoma.

Watching my father cry, I held back tears in my eyes and prayed and encouraged him.

Days later, my father called me hysterically crying, saying that the doctors had given him two weeks to live. Once again, I was left in a position to contact my family to come to the hospital. Due to my father being so private and so hurt, I was left to tell my sisters, brother, aunts, and uncles that the doctors had given him two weeks to live. I went back to the room and declared life, peace, strength, and love over my father and my family. In December 2018, I became my father's primary caregiver by default and at his request. Not only did I care for my father, but I watched him die right before my eyes. Holding firm to my faith and praying with my father, I could not believe that I was watching him slowly leave me. Once again, I had to muster up great strength to care for someone who did not even do half of what I did for them. For months I not only had to deal with my own medical condition but also care for my father, two paternal grandmothers, and a maternal grandfather.

One thing I learned during that encounter was to pray without ceasing. I prayed with my father day in and day out; I encouraged him while I was encouraging myself. We grew strong together in our faith, and I'll always hold dear how we built a close relationship with each other. I did attend grief counseling after losing my father, and I am currently seeing a therapist/counselor to help me navigate through family/friends relationships and life in general.

Chapter 6: Being Equipped!...or Know When to Humble Yourself!

In 2019, I truly had an encounter with God; it was uncommon and unique! I graduated with my Master's Degree from Wilmington University and lost my father and one of my paternal grandmothers. I literally had to humble myself in so many areas of my life to overcome impenetrable situations. I had no job nor any source of income for the majority of 2018 and 2019. There were moments when my own family and friends were defaming my character with fallacious info. However, I decided to cut out all the unnecessary "noise" and hear from God. Overall, my year was bittersweet, BUT One thing I never lost during this process was how to TRUST God. Although my faith waivered at times, I kept going and discovered that I was and still am VERY STRONG. I prayed daily and stood firm on God's Word while speaking affirmations over my life... Romans 8:18, Romans 8:28, Psalms 37:25, and John 14:1.

I found myself in a deep struggle both mentally and emotionally. After my father passed on April 12, 2019, so many complex things occurred pertaining to his death. The most challenging thing when planning a service is selecting a casket and spray. Visualizing my father in a casket was something I was not prepared to do, yet I knew I was equipped to handle the task. During the week of planning and preparation, my family had to ensure my father had clothes all the way down to his underwear, a haircut, and a final resting place. Making a huge decision, or should I say preparing for a major assignment, was not easy. Whenever doing something for the first time, you never know what the end result will be; however, you hope and pray for a positive outcome. It's sad to say that there was little support because of the rumors and false accusations made by others. It appeared to be a battle with our own adversary due to the lack trust. I was glad that those who were willing and able to help put their feelings to the side and did what was best for my father. People came from other states to funeralize my father with such class, integrity, and grace.

Months went by, and I tell you I had to humble myself because I was facing great embarrassment to the point of being humiliated. In June 2019, I was sitting on my bed in tears because I had no money. I literally did not even have 20 cents to purchase a pack of noodles. I found myself saving half empty water bottles just so I could have something to drink throughout the day. With no hope and feeling defeated, I sat on my bed and cried out to God, pleading on what I should do next. I had used all of the money in my bank accounts, which were eventually closed, and had no other resources. After wiping my tears, I got up, took a shower, and got dressed. I gathered up some strength with tears flooding my eyes and falling down my face; I found myself at the Burlington County Board of Social Services building (Welfare Office), applying for assistance. Again, feeling humiliated and embarrassed, I walked up to the desk and whispered to the clerk, "I am here to apply for assistance." She gave me a stack of papers to complete, and with a hoodie over my head, I completed the forms to the best of my ability. After waiting for an hour to hear them say, "Number 103," I got up and went to the rear offices and met with the attendant. She asked why I was there; I responded, "Because I have no job, no income, and no food."

She then said okay, "You're in an Emergency situation?"

I said, "Pretty much."

The attendant proceeded to ask me the routine questions. She then said, "You will hear something back from your assigned case manager within a few weeks."

Later that day, I called my best friend Yah. While holding back tears, I explained to him what was going on. He said, "Tee, do not worry about it; I got you." He came by my house and said, "Let's go to Wal-Mart and get you some stuff." ANYONE who knows me knows that I love Wal-Mart and that I live in that store. Being who I am, I only got a few items because I knew he was a single man, living on his own, and trying to save his money. I was so appreciative for just the little thing that I was able to make the food stretch for a few days.

The following week was our church's annual POG convocation. During that week there were various sessions that took place. I signed up for the ones that I needed the most during my difficult time, just to name a few: How to overcome doubt and fear, How to minister to those when you are lost yourself, and How to get through challenging situations. I was feeling a little refreshed although I was still broken on the inside. That Thursday afternoon, Pastor John F. Hannah preached the mid-day service and told us to form a circle with our neighbors. He said I am giving you all three numbers and you can decide which one you want to be amongst yourselves. We assembled ourselves, and I decided to go second. I said, "I will be Two"—not knowing this was the number that was going to speak life into my situation. As Pastor John Hannah called out each number, he told the person to stand in the middle while the other two formed a circle around them to pray. Well, he mentioned, "Now Number Two, you get in the middle," and when I tell you he said, "FORSAKEN…... I have never seen the righteous forsaken nor seed begging bread (Psalms 37:25)," I lost it. Pastor Hannah began to say that the secret petitions of our hearts (Psalms 37), the desires and secrets of your heart, and delight yourself in the Lord. I was crying hysterically because I was in a place that I honestly thought God had forsaken me, but He sent me a confirmation that He had not left my side. Pastor Hannah also said, "Stay in the Press." I cried for the remainder of the afternoon while worshipping God.

Throughout the year, there were people who would randomly sow into my life financially: my brothers (Marcel, Pee, and Jayson) and my sisters (Bonnie, Rylee, Tashia, Ivory, Branea, and Da'Mo). There were many times when Momma Clementine would say, "Follow me after church" and take me to the store to purchase food for my home. Momma Clementine would encourage me and pray with me to uplift my spirits. Even in my lowest, when I did not want to pray, she would send me a text with a prayer. God sent me some special angels like Colleen and Darren; I call them my Aunt and Uncle. They were and still are tremendously supportive in my life. I call Colleen my family's primary doctor because she has gotten us through some difficult health scares. She remained consistent and loyal to my family when my grandmothers, father, and even myself became ill. Without Colleen, I would not have obtained so much knowledge medically during this journey.

Okay, back to my journey... Later that week, I received a noticed from Social Services that I was approved for temporary services for both food and cash assistance. I immediately became grateful and praised God, but I was wondering, "How did I get into such a challenging place that I need welfare assistance?" I heard God loud and clear, and He said, "Trust My Process." Still embarrassed, I went down and obtained my EBT card. I went home, looked over on my bookshelf and noticed *Healed Without Scars* by Bishop Evans, the book I had previously read. This time I knew I needed to read it again from a different angle of spiritual growth and maturity.

After searching and applying for jobs for almost a year, on July 25, 2019, I was able to obtain employment again because of two great people: Colleen and Darren. They were able to contact one of their friends who owned a company. I met with the owner, Jim, and he hired me on the spot. He asked me if I could start work the following Tuesday, which was July 30, 2019. I was truly appreciative because of the opportunity that had been presented to me. I was now able to receive income again. Anyone who knows me knows that I love to provide for myself and dread asking others for any kind of help or assistance.

In September 2019, my pastor Bishop Evans taught a message, "According to Your Faith" (Matthew 4:1-6). He said faith is not influenced by time, but God gives us faith to handle time. He mentioned that time does not control seasons, so if I miss a season, I know that it is coming around again. He taught from Acts 3:16: "and through faith in the name of Jesus, the cripple man was healed." So, what I learned is, if I want the impossible to happen, I must have faith and be surrounded by people who believe that my blessing will come to pass.

Many times, I felt like Job when God allowed Satan to test him more than once (Job 1:6 and Job 2:1). I felt like I was stripped to nothing after facing various tests, challenges, and struggles, one after another. No matter what, Job spoke highly of God and remained in prayer. In the end, God gave him twice as much as he had lost. When I lost my job, grandmothers, and father, I asked God, "What have I done wrong to deal with so many great losses?"

I even felt like Moses when God instructed him to lead the people out of Egypt (Exodus 3:10-13 and Exodus 4:1-17). Although what God was showing me was right in my possession, I doubted him because of fear and insecurity. There was a situation that I was in due to the loss of a loved one. I faced great opposition with no support from my family and friends. Bishop Evans said at a Wednesday Bible Study, "Whatever you need is right in front of your face, and you have the power to complete whatever task." I immediately looked at Momma Pearl who said, "I told you; you got this!" I knew I had it, but I was not confident enough to believe God had equipped me for this next assignment. I decided to Trust God; do not get me wrong, my faith waivered at times! What I realized at the time was that God was trying to show me His capacity like He showed Moses. The following week Bishop Evans said something so profound during his series *Armed and Dangerous*: "If we are going to fight, we might as well WIN." I knew it was my season to win this battle.

At times I thought I was the woman with the issue of blood who was just trying to get close to Jesus for her healing. Luke 8:43 talks about a woman in the crowd who had suffer bleeding for twelve years. The woman could find no cure, so she was determined to just touch Jesus for her healing, and because of her faith, she was made whole. On several occasions, I was just rushing to feel God in my presence.

Chapter 7: Am I Built for This?

Around December 2019, I felt a throbbing on the left side of my body. I ignored the pain and assumed it was due to the anxiety and stress I had experienced throughout the year. Well, in January 2020, it was to the point that my left foot was swelling up at times. So, I called Colleen who I consider to be my personal doctor (lol). Colleen told me to take some Tylenol and Advil. She also advised me to elevate my leg at night with a pillow. Well, that only worked for a short period of time. A few weeks went by, and it was on/off pins and needles irritation. Finally, after Bible Study on March 4, 2020, I went to Urgent Care to avoid going to the Emergency Room because the ER wait was over an hour, and the doctor treated me for inflammation, swelling, and Neuritis. I had to take steroids for seven days, which again only helped temporarily. Fast forward to March 11, 2020, a week later; I finally went to the Emergency Room where they instructed me to contact my Primary Care Physician (PCP). Therefore, I followed-up with my PCP on March 18, 2020; I met with my doctor who had great concern because my left side appeared to be weaker than the right side. As a result, she scheduled an MRI of my brain on March 31, 2020.

Welp… the doctor emailed me on Thursday, April 2, 2020, which sent me into an emotional state; however, this time I began to worship and cry out to God. I started to speak healing and great health over my life. I texted a few family members and friends for them to agree with me in prayer. The doctor then called me about an hour later and was very concerned about my MRI results and mentioned that I had Idiopathic Intracranial Hypertension. She asked me to contact an ophthalmologist for them to do further testing of my vision and brain. I'm not going to lie—I was both fearful and prayerful at the same time. I had heard the news earlier that day that my great-aunt DeeDee, who was dear to me, had died. I felt like there was no end to bad news.

God knows what He is doing because on April 2, 2020, while I was sitting at my desk, I received random text messages from people stating that God had laid me on their hearts. So, one of my spiritual brothers, Marcel (Twin), said he had been taking Communion with his church and wanted to encourage me to join them. I started taking Communion as an "Act of Intercession" and really believed God for the impossible and the miraculous. I really started thanking God for Marcel because there was a time I would have reacted in total fear and added more negativity to the situation I was experiencing. I started taking Holy Communion daily, consecrated myself to read God's Word and pray daily, and decreed and declared both Psalms 46 and Psalms 103 over my life.

❖ Psalm 46 King James Version (KJV)

God is our refuge and strength, a very present help in trouble. [2]Therefore will not we fear, though the earth be removed, and though the mountains be carried into the midst of the sea; [3]Though the waters thereof roar and be troubled, though the mountains shake with the swelling thereof. Selah. [4]There is a river, the streams whereof shall make glad the city of God, the holy place of the tabernacles of the most High. [5]God is in the midst of her; she shall not be moved: God shall help her, and that right early. [6]The heathen raged, the kingdoms were moved: he uttered his voice, the earth melted. [7]The Lord of hosts is with us; the

God of Jacob is our refuge. Selah. [8]Come, behold the works of the Lord, what desolations he hath made in the earth. [9]He maketh wars to cease unto the end of the earth; he breaketh the bow, and cutteth the spear in sunder; he burneth the chariot in the fire. [10]Be still and know that I am God: I will be exalted among the heathen; I will be exalted in the earth. [11]The Lord of hosts is with us; the God of Jacob is our refuge. Selah.

> Psalm 103 King James Version (KJV)

Bless the Lord, O my soul: and all that is within me, bless his holy name. [2]Bless the Lord, O my soul, and forget not all his benefits: [3]Who forgiveth all thine iniquities; who healeth all thy diseases; [4]Who redeemeth thy life from destruction; who crowneth thee with lovingkindness and tender mercies; [5]Who satisfieth thy mouth with good things; so that thy youth is renewed like the eagle's. [6]The Lord executeth righteousness and judgment for all that are oppressed. [7]He made known his ways unto Moses, his acts unto the children of Israel. [8]The Lord is merciful and gracious, slow to anger, and plenteous in mercy. [9]He will not always chide: neither will he keep his anger forever. [10]He hath not dealt with us after our sins; nor rewarded us according to our iniquities. [11]For as the heaven is high above the earth, so great is his mercy toward them that fear him. *12As far as the east is from the west, so far hath he removed our transgressions from us. 13Like as a father pitieth his children, so the Lord pitieth them that fear him. 14For he knoweth our frame; he remembereth that we are dust. 15As for man, his days are as grass: as a flower of the field, so he flourisheth. 16For the wind passeth over it, and it is gone; and the place thereof shall know it no more. 17But the mercy of the Lord is from everlasting to everlasting upon them that fear him, and his righteousness unto children's children; 18To such as keep his covenant, and to those that remember his commandments to do them. 19The Lord hath prepared his throne in the heavens; and his kingdom ruleth overall. 20Bless the Lord, ye his angels, that excel in strength, that do his commandments, hearkening unto the voice of his word. 21Bless ye the Lord, all ye his hosts; ye ministers of his, that do his pleasure. 22Bless the Lord, all his works in all places of his dominion: bless the Lord, O my soul.*

April 21, 2020, I attended my initial appointment with Dr. Russell (ophthalmologist) at Wills Eyes Hospital and walked into that doctor's office fearless. The doctor asked me if I had been dealing with any vision loss, stress, or trauma recently. I expressed to the doctor (with tears falling down my face) how I had been dealing with a lot of stress regarding the loss of my father. The doctor reviewed my paperwork and conducted the first part of my exam. I wiped my eyes with a tissue so that she could finish the first portion of the exam. The doctor left, and one of the assistants came in to start the next phase of the exam. This was a three-part process, and then, finally, I could hear them whispering in the hall about my results. The head doctor said, "Hmm…I see." After reviewing my charts, my exam results, and speaking with the assistant, the head doctor finally came in with the concluding results. When Dr. Russell (the Head Specialist) walked in, I looked at him and the assistant and stated, "I don't want to hear anything but a GOOD report."

He turned around and looked at me with a stern look and said, "Well, Ms. Gee, all is well." Then, he proceeded to conduct his portion of the test, and once he finished, he said, "How much weight have you gained in the past two years?" I said about fifteen to twenty pounds due to stress and anxiety. He said, "Well, all your test came back NORMAL, and it looks like what is happening is your spinal cord is not producing the correct amount of fluid to your brain which is causing pressure." He stated that he wanted me to lose weight and come back within the next four months to see if I had made any progress.

After I left the appointment, I got onto the elevator and pressed the button for the first floor. Once I got off the elevator, I went outside of the hospital and began to walk down Walnut Street in Philadelphia; I began to praise God because it could have gone another way. I realized once I increased my FAITH to believe and trust GOD's process that in the end, ALL WILL BE WELL. Once I got back to my car, I grabbed my phone and immediately called my family and my friends and provided them with the praise report. I was determined to live, so I decided to do some things for myself, such as purchase a new bed, eat healthy foods, and exercise daily.

Part 3: Winning

Chapter 8: I Shall Live Testimony

April 22, 2020, I started my new journey and started exercising daily. I began by making smoothies, eating more fruits and vegetables, along with cutting carbohydrates. I realized that my FAITH had to be increased during this season. I was even GRATEFUL because when I revisited my life a year prior, I had literally been facing a car repossession and an eviction notice. I am so appreciative because even during a worldwide pandemic, I still have my car, my job, and a place to live. I realized that in the midst of this COVID-19/Coronavirus, God had sustained my life.

While talking to one of my friends (Yah), I reminisced that over a year ago, I was quarantined involuntarily due to what I had experienced with the loss of my father, job, and finances. I started explaining to Yah how thankful I was because God had spread his Grace and Mercy over my life. I began to remind Yah how a year ago, I was so secluded from everyone and felt so defeated, yet God saw fit to continue to make provisions for me throughout the process. We had a dialogue about how AMAZING God is and how he does things so WELL. Looking back, I would have never thought I would had been able to surpass the position I was in. BUT GOD, He vindicated my life, saw my needs, and continued/continues to BLESS me over and over again.

I joined a few pastors' weekly prayers and Bible studies through various social channels during the pandemic. Often, I would call in to my church's "Noon-day Prayer" conference call. Every Wednesday, I attended my church Bethany Baptist/Bishop David G. Evans' Facebook Live. Every Tuesday from 6:00 p.m. to 7:00 p.m., I joined Mt. Moriah Pentecostal Church/Pastor Mary Clark for a conference call prayer. On Thursdays, I would engage in Pastor John F. Hannah's Facebook Live Bible study or prayer broadcast. I connected to New Life Church/Pastor John F. Hannah's Facebook Live.

I am forever grateful to God for all the many blessings that He has bestowed upon my life. I was able to increase my relationship with God; I prayed daily, fasted often, study the Word (Bible), listened to gospel music, and just meditated in His presence. There was never a moment that I did not take the time to offer a sweet reverence praise unto God.

Chapter 9: Chosen!

On May 12, 2020, I received an email from the Nashholt Hospice Counselor. He wanted to know if I was interested in speaking to the "doctoring class" and providing them with a narrative regarding my grieving process and the experience with my father's care. Mr. Holden provided me with a detailed email of the expectations from me as a family member. The email explained that the session will begin with an interview of me as the bereaved family member of a hospice patient. I would be paired with a bereavement/hospice counselor (Mrs. Adar). I, as the family member, would be supported by the hospice worker and would share my personal narrative to open a dialog with the students regarding end-of-life care, bereavement, and bereavement care. Mr. Holden mentioned how every year the Franchisco School of Medicine (of

Nashholt Medicine) hosts a special class for medical students that is designed to help train newer doctors in how to best serve patients and families when they are at the end of life/on hospice and how best to support grieving families during the early portions of their bereavement experience.

Mr. Holden pointed out how this year the class would be held virtually (via a platform like BlueJeans or Zoom), and it would be on Tuesday, June 2, 2020, from 2:05 p.m. to 2:50 p.m. A family member who has experienced the loss of a loved one under the hospice service is asked to tell his or her story to the class (for about 20-30 minutes) and to then field questions from the class (for about 15-20 minutes). He had attached the type of questions that the students were encouraged to ask me. He stated that the heart of the class is really the individual's personal story of love, loss, grief, and healing—and how the medical profession can better serve patients and families at the end of life, when on hospice, and during the early portions of their grief experiences. Below is the email that was addressed to me:

Tori, I would like to invite you to be a participant in this experience if you would be so inclined. Your sensitivity, your capacity for self-expression and the wisdom that you have gleaned from your grief experience is evident ... And – while grief is an on-going process – I believe that you may be at a place to tell your story in a way that could be helpful for others to hear. Only, you yourself, however, really knows if that is true for you at this time. However, I would like to offer you the opportunity to share your story with these students, if it feels like something that you would wish to do.

There are several things to consider:

> ➢ *It will be a virtual classroom (so you will need to have some technical capacity for navigating a platform that involves audio and visual pieces) as well as a laptop or desktop that will allow for that.*

> ➢ *You would be asked to speak for 20-25 minutes and allow 15-20 minutes for questions from the medical students and providing answers to those questions.*

> ➢ *You would have one of our psychosocial staff "accompany" you (virtually). That is either myself or another grief counselor or social worker or chaplain will be "with" you to introduce you and to provide support for you and to facilitate any questions that the class might ask. So, you would not be doing this "alone" so to speak.*

On Tuesday, June 2, 2020, I was able to elaborate on my relationships with my father's physicians and how they were supportive and understanding of what my family and I had to deal with. I logged into the Zoom ("BlueJeans") meeting around 1:50 p.m. because I was so anxious about telling my story to the students. As the minutes went by, more and more participants joined the meeting. As I saw each face appear on the screen, I became more confident in telling my story. Around 2:05 p.m., Mrs. Dakota the coordinator began to introduce me to the class. As I watched sixteen (16) other faces appear on the screen, it was now my turn to speak.

I started to expound on my father's end-of-life care and the supports that were provided for me and my grieving family. I told them that it was incredibly challenging to watch as a daughter, especially because my father wanted to LIVE. I showed the doctoring class a picture of my father in his cream blazer and blue top with his chocolate round face and innocent smirk. I specified how the word "hospice" can be exceedingly difficult for family members to process, knowing there is a 90% chance the family member will not live beyond six months. I provided the team with the ways I cope with my father's death—for example, I listen to his favorite songs: "I'll Be Missing You" by Puff Daddy, "Optimistic" by The Sound of Blackness, and "The Moment" by Kenny G. I also visit my father's gravesite; I sit and cry, listen to music, and place artificial blue, white, or burgundy flowers or "DAD" arrangements. I told them how I look at our family pictures and just reminisce on the good times and even bad times. I talked about how I had to learn how to care for my father by asking the doctors questions, taking notes, and comparing the previous ones, communicating with active family members, and talking to my nurse-friend. It was not easy to educate myself on medical terminology, how to operate a peripherally inserted central catheter, and flush an Intravenous therapy (IV line). It was such a huge responsibility, but because of my faith in God, I knew I was equipped for the task.

It felt good to grasp everyone's attention while telling my story. They seemed to be intrigued and interested in what I had to say during the virtual interview, especially because some of them were shaking their heads and showing faces of concern as I was speaking. After my portion of the session, Mrs. Adar was able to give her perspective as a counselor and how younger children cope with losing a parent. She explained that it is important for the counselors to be blunt and straight forward about the parent's end-of-life care. Mrs. Adar stated that many children do not know how to comprehend and feel guilty about losing a parent, especially at a young age. The interview lasted about 45 minutes from (2:05 p.m. - 2:50 p.m.) and was conducted by two students from the group.

Chapter 10: Who Am I? What Am I Doing?...Confused

Still trying to figure out who I was, I found myself doing things to fill an empty void in my life. Although I was still going to church, praying, reading my Bible, and praising God, I still felt purposeless. I decided that I was going to start smoking weed, drinking wine, and having sex so that I could hide from reality. Life became so complicated and so convoluted I got so caught up in my mess.

L. A. T. O. R. I. A.

My Negative Emotions: Lonely, Anxious, Threatened, Overwhelmed, Rejected, Isolated, Alienated/Apathetic

My Positive Emotions: Loving, Amazing, Triumphant, Optimistic, Revived, Innovative, Assured

Due to my asthma, from which I was trying to protect myself, I began eating "edible" treats. I would have an edible treat to soothe my feelings and emotions. One day, I could not wait to eat a Red Velvet edible; I had even put cream cheese icing on it to make it a little more flavorful to eat. Let me be honest…the edibles helped calm down the emotional distress I was experiencing at the time. I remember one time eating a cookie at a party; at first, I did not know what I was eating. Once I realized what was in the cookie and the effect it had on me, I knew at that point it was something I was not supposed to be doing. It was so bad, to the point that I called one of my friends (Ez) and said, "Something is wrong with me, and I think they are trying to kill me." My friend Ez instructed me to go back into the house and wait to leave until the effect was no longer strong in my system. All I could think was, "If I had driven home at that moment, I was going to end up in a ditch somewhere." I decided to stay at the house where the party was until I was able to go home. That was the last time for that type of situation.

Drinking would come as needed, but it was not as intense as the edibles. I would go to the local Mt. Ever liquor store to grab either a 4-pack of Kahlua & Cream, 6-pack of Smirnoff Ice Flavor Coolers, a 750ml bottle of Grey Goose, or a 750ml bottle of Svedka Vodka Strawberry Lemonade. I would typically purchase six-packs because it was less alcohol. One day I remember standing in the store embarrassed about my alcohol purchase, knowing it was something I was not supposed to be getting myself into. As I stood in the line looking around the store to make sure I did not see anyone familiar, I proceeded to the check-out counter. The cashier scanned my six-pack and asked me if I wanted a receipt. I immediately said, "No" because I did not want the check-out process to take any longer.

Sex: what was it to me? It was a feeling of being loved in a moment that I never thought I would get back. It was a sensation to get me through an emotion, to not feel lonely. No, I was not randomly having sexual intercourse with various people; it was only one person. Do not get me wrong... when I had sexual intercourse, I was always convicted afterwards because I knew it was something that I was not supposed to be doing. I was not married, and because of the Biblical teachings, I knew it was wrong. However, this one time, I was extremely guilty afterwards; I cried so much that I shut down. I prayed and asked God to really deliver me and heal my mind from the thoughts of having sexual intercourse. I searched through my Bible application to seek scriptures to help me not want that feeling any longer.

➤ Ephesians 5:1-5 King James Version (KJV)
Be ye therefore followers of God, as dear children; ²And walk in love, as Christ also hath loved us, and hath given himself for us an offering and a sacrifice to God for a sweet smelling savour. ³But fornication, and all uncleanness, or covetousness, let it not be once named among you, as becometh saints; ⁴Neither filthiness, nor foolish talking, nor

jesting, which are not convenient: but rather giving of thanks. [5]For this ye know, that no whoremonger, nor unclean person, nor covetous man, who is an idolater, hath any inheritance in the kingdom of Christ and of God.

After a while, the fix would only be temporary for me because once the high, buzz, or sex was over, life was still present. I realized that I still had to face reality. I recall praying to myself, saying "This is not what I am supposed to be doing." I had standards that I needed to uphold myself to, especially because I let them down for an interim fix. I had sisters and other females who were watching me, and I needed to get myself together to lead by example. It was not fair to them nor was it beneficial for me to act in an ungodly manner whenever I faced a crisis. I had to show them and exhibit what it took to maintain my strength and potency when feeling weak and worthless. Although I was still trying to figure out my purpose, I was not going to allow a short setback to dictate my future. Overall, those experiences taught me that life happens, hindrances occur, and stumbling blocks appear, but I have to keep my head up and keep running the course. I was at a point that I honestly did not know who I was and/or who I was becoming. I remember one day my sister Tashia said to me, "I have never known you to eat edibles, drink, or talk about struggling with sex."

My response to my sister was, "You all never allowed me to live in my truth." As the oldest sister, I always had to wear a mask and was never able to be totally honest about my issues and my inner weaknesses. I explained to my sister that I was human and that I had many faults like she did, but the problem was people did not give me the opportunity to be true to myself. My family had high expectations for me, which in return caused me to live up to a higher demand. So, for many years, I was not able to live life with who Latoria really was/is.

Chapter 11: Self-Focused: Set Apart...Don't Get Caught Up in the Mix

As I reclaimed my joy and peace, I discovered "Latoria Gee." I had lived my life making huge sacrifices for others—family, friends, coworkers, and associates. I had neglected myself and lost focused on whom I was ordained and called to be. I am now at a place, when and where, I can be content with the decisions I make and not think twice about other people's opinions. I used to worry about if people would get upset with me if I said "No" to them. I was always a "Yes" person and put myself last or not at all. I literally took the clothes off my back to make sure others were okay; to think about it, those same people would not even give me a hot meal when I was close to losing everything I had. I have learned how to say "No" and not feel bad about what I could not do for others.

I had to understand that I played a part in my healing process, but I also needed to take responsibility for my actions, as well. In life, I tended to blame others and blame God for the consequences of the decisions I made. I can be honest and say that I participated in some things that I should not have indulged in at such a young age. Once I started taking ownership of who I was, I noticed changes in my responses to people, my characteristics, and my attitude.

In February 2020, I decided to reinstate my gym membership and focus on my health. I noticed during my complex season that I lost who I was, became depressed, and started gaining weight— maybe about 15-20 pounds. I became an emotional eater, and instead of facing my reality, I turned to comfort food to feel better in the moment. When I went to see my primary care physician Doctor Mamie, she told me that I weighed over 220 pounds; I immediately became embarrassed and was determined to focus on the new me. It was time for my new beginning. This time was different than before. I realized I had a habit of saying I was going to change, but it was only for a certain period.

I started going to the gym, eating healthier, and began to feel good again. I had my joy back and obtained the peace I was looking for. I was now preparing myself to be in the position to receive what God had in stored for me. I was excited about volunteering at my church on various ministries, as well. I was grateful for the opportunity to help someone else get through what I had experienced. Each of the ministries were/are precious to me, and I value what I did/do to support others. Below is a brief synopsis of the ministries I was/am a part of:

* **No Longer Bound**: Focused on domestic violence and how to empower victims to be free from all types of abuse. I was excited to be a part of the ministry because I have a heart to help others and to encourage them to utilize positive coping strategies. I feel good about advocating for victims to obtain the power to protect themselves.

* **The People:** Centered around helping those who are in nursing homes. I enjoy the ministry because I visit family members, friends, and those I know who are unwell. I spend time with individuals who are currently either residing in the nursing homes or sick in the hospitals daily. I love just sitting with those individuals who are ill because the experience is remarkable, knowing that just spending

time with someone makes them feel better and puts a smile on their face.

* **Outstretching Hands:** I love volunteering to serve others. I find pleasure in collaborating with other people who can assist with ensuring there are positive and effective outcomes relating to the needs of others. When I volunteer, it is totally incredible to see the impact that we, as a church, have on the community.

* **Extending my Vocals**: Singing is very therapeutic for me and is an opportunity to express my gratification to God, while yet encouraging someone else through song. I have been singing since I was a little girl, from the age of 5-years-old. I know my powerful alto voice can deliver someone out of a circumstance.

* **Teaching our Youth:** Young people are very charismatic and haughty. There is nothing like the feeling of talking to someone younger than you and knowing that your words will change his/her future. I enjoy providing words of wisdom and purpose, especially for those I know who could have successful futures.

* **Outside the Barriers**: This ministry really inspired me because I previously worked in the Human Services field and learned that there are plenty of resources and supports

for everyone in need. This ministry is very distinctive to me because I know I can support someone in an area I was able to overcome and exceed. There is nothing like feeling good about supporting someone and knowing that he/she has received the resources to surpass his/her current crisis.

Overall, it is truly a blessing to serve and an honor to be chosen by God to be in a position to support many people within the community. Anyone who knows me knows that I love giving, supporting, serving, and encouraging others. My goal is to have a positive impact on everyone I encounter. I want to ensure people's lives are changed for the better after I have been in connection with them. I want people to feel empowered, inspired, and confident that they can become and do anything they put their hearts and minds into. However, I discovered that I cannot be on a mission and not experience warfare.

As I move forward in this next journey, I am positioning myself for what God has planned for my latter days of the years to come! Stay tuned! Every day I grab my bottle of "Holy Oil," and I declare and decree over my life the blessings God has for me. I use my shower-time to talk to God; the water is so refreshing and gives me a sense of peace, silence, and calmness. I speak daily affirmations over my life, such as "I am healed"…"I am an overcomer"…"I am successful"…"I am strong"…"I am delivered"…"I am BLESSED"…"I am encouraged"…"I am healthy"…"I am wealthy"…"I am the head"…"I am above"…"I am the lender"…"I am anointed"…"I am talented"…"I am gifted"…"I am empowered"…"I am FAVORED"…"I am uniquely different"…"I am uniquely the same"…"I am positioned"…"I am EQUIPPED and designed for the rest of my life."

I will leave you with this: Stay true to yourself, maintain integrity, and keep GOD first. I know God has given me the ability to drive out and overcome every adversary. My energy has been increased; my strength has been built, and the promise has been released over my life. This is not the END! I am living in my Ephesians 3:20 (AMEN).

Chapter 12: My Future is Blessed

Starting on June 1, 2020, I decided to speak declarations, encouragement, and affirmations over my month. Let us take a look at how these daily words kept me going…

❖ *June 2020*

- *STRENGTH*: I needed strength at a time when and where I was at my weakest. The scripture I stood by was 1 Peter 5:10 (NIV): *And the God of all grace,*

who called you to his eternal glory in Christ, after
you have suffered a little while, will himself restore
you and make you strong, firm and steadfast.

❖ *July 2020*

- *PEACE:* There was so much chaos going on in my
  life that I was searching for peace. I studied the
  following scripture and applied it to my life: John
  14:27 (NIV*) Peace I leave with you; my peace I*
  give you. I do not give to you as the world gives. Do
  not let your hearts be troubled and do not be afraid.

❖ *August 2020*

- *WISDOM*: During the month of August, I noticed
  that I needed to make some crucial decisions that
  were essential for the next season in my life. As I
  prayed and search for a scripture to stand firm on, I
  came across Ecclesiastes 8:1 (TLV): *Who is like the*
  wise person? Who knows the meaning of a matter?
  A person's wisdom makes his face shine,
  transforming the harshness of his face.

❖ *September 2020*

- ***POWER & AUTHORITY***: As I moved on to each month, speaking life into my situations, I became more confident that God was my Provider. I read two scriptures during the month of September: Isaiah 40:29 & 2 Peter 1:3.
  - o Isaiah 40:29 (NLT): *He gives power to the weak and strength to the powerless.*
  - o 2 Peter 1:3 (NLT): *By his divine power, God has given us everything we need for living a godly life. We have received all of this by coming to know him, the one who called us to himself by means of his marvelous glory and excellence.*

- ❖ ***October 2020***
  - ***JOY***: I was determined to live in my happiness. For a long time, I dwelt in so much sadness and sorrow. I wanted to finally delight in God's path for my life. I was now a survivor of my own "self." I recited three scriptures for the month and spoke them over my life:
    - o Psalm 16:11 (AMP): *You will show me the path of life; In Your presence is fullness of*

joy; In Your right hand there are pleasures forevermore.

- o Romans 15:13 (KJV): *Now the God of hope fill you with all joy and peace in believing, that ye may abound in hope, through the power of the Holy Ghost.*
- o Colossians 1:11 (CEV): *His glorious power will make you patient and strong enough to endure anything, and you will be truly happy.*

❖ *November 2020*

- *VICTORIOUS*: With life and death being in the power of the words that we speak daily, I commanded Victory. I always win because I am on God's side. I stood firm on two scriptures for my winning season. I proclaimed triumph for the rest of my life:
  - o Psalm 44: 6-8 (NIV): *I put no trust in my bow, my sword does not bring me victory; [7]but you give us victory over our enemies, you put our adversaries to shame. [8]In God we make our boast all day long, and we will praise your name forever.*

- o Psalm 118: 6-7 (ESV): *The Lord is on my side; I will not fear. What can man do to me? ⁷The Lord is on my side as my helper; I shall look in triumph on those who hate me.*

❖ *December 2020*

- • *JUSTICE:* There is nothing like the feeling of justice, righteousness, equitableness, or moral rightness. I have struggled for many years with receiving justice because of other people's opinions, behaviors, and actions regarding me. I just want peace, equality, and genuine respect from other people. Below are a few scriptures I applied during my month:
  - o Psalm 89:14 (TLB): *Your throne is founded on two strong pillars—the one is Justice and the other Righteousness. Mercy and Truth walk before you as your attendants.*
  - o Luke 18:6-8 (ESV): *And the Lord said, "Hear what the unrighteous judge says. ⁷And will not God give justice to his elect, who cry to him day and night? Will he delay long over them? ⁸I tell you, he will give justice to them speedily. Nevertheless,*

when the Son of Man comes, will he find
faith on earth?"

For the rest of the year, I decreed and declared that my October, November, and December would be blessed along with everything attached to me. I remember listening to Pastor John F. Hannah one particular Sunday in September, and he stated, "Suddenly, things will begin to turn because of the Suffering." Pastor Hannah also instructed us (Facebook Live viewers) to speak over our next three months. He expressed how our next three months were going to be better than our previous twenty years. He also mentioned how what was being held would soon be released. I began to receive everything he professed upon my life.

I appreciate my Godson's parents, Ivy & Rickey, for blessing me with the book *Promises from God's Heart* by DaySpring. This book has been a blessing to me because it helps me with comforting truths for my every need daily. I turn to this book daily for uplifting and encouraging scriptures. Whenever I need a Word to get me through a particular situation, I search through the content page and retrieve whatever topic I need to study a scripture for. I have truly learned how to apply the pressure during God's process.

My Gratitude

I am truly grateful to God for allowing me to experience this journey because I know it wasn't just for me but to help someone else. God, You have truly been a Way-maker in my time of trouble and suffering, my Strength when I am weak, my Provider when I do not have, and just my All-in-all. I now understand why You, God, permitted so many obstacles to occur in my life. You knew I was destined and equipped to win this journey. I value the times that I had to cry, fight, and force myself through challenges. However, looking back, God, You were there with me every step of the way. God, You positioned and equipped me to have various encounters with You. As I reminisce on this unique journey called LIFE, You have never forsaken me. Although there were times when I felt alone, I appreciate You because You were there the entire time. God, I thank You for Your son Jesus-Christ's dying for the sins that I struggle with daily. I would be nothing without my ultimate relationship with You. I am forever honored to be called Your daughter and the chosen one.

I appreciate my mother, Victoria Vernae, for her wisdom and her love for God. Mom, I value your courage and your ability to support everyone in your family. We agree to disagree at times, but I understand your viewpoint as a mother and as a woman of God. I am grateful that you instilled in me the ability to obtain integrity and respect no matter how other people treat me. Mom, you might not have been able to support me financially like you wanted to, but you always provide me with words of encouragement, motivation, and knowledge. I find myself behaving like you at times. You exhibit such great skillsets. However, no one would ever know that you are broken inside because you always want people to see the strength that you carry. I learned from you that it is okay to be transparent, ambitious, and still be strong. In the end, nothing or no one can take away the gifts and anointings that God has instilled in you. I am grateful for the daily conversations that we have; however, sometimes I do believe you like to challenge me to reveal my inner powers. Although at times you appear to be insensitive and critical, I know you always want to see the best in me. I honestly appreciate you, and I love you; your willpower admonishes me to keep going!

I appreciate my father, Robert Kenneth (may he continue to rest). Dad, you taught me patience and pulled out my inner strengths. Looking back, it was nothing but the Grace of God that I was able to gather the tenacity to sacrifice my life to care for someone who had not done half for me of what I did for him in two years. Dad, your love was different, and I had to understand that you were a product of your environment. I had to look past your absence and be grateful for the time and opportunity that I had to spend with you. My spiritual walk was challenged when you were diagnosed with colon adenocarcinoma. There was nothing like hearing the doctors communicate that there was nothing they could do for you to be cured of this disease. Watching the look of defeat on your face, along with knowing the fear of tomorrow, indeed broke my heart. However, I was determined to speak life to your situation. I was tested at a level I never thought God would put me on. I prayed, fasted, and sacrificed my time to ensure you received the support you needed. Dad, all you wanted was to be completely healed in your physical body; you wanted to live. However, God had other plans…. That is what church people say, right? However, what I am grateful most for was that I was able to relate to you on a different level when it came to various areas of my life. We were able to build a relationship that many daughters never get a chance to do with absent fathers. Let me make this clear… Although you were not a part of my lift consistently as a child, when I got old enough, we were able to establish a connection and an unbreakable bond. I would go over to your house just to watch the Eagles game, go to dinner, or just to spend time with you. You will truly be missed, Dad, and I cherish every memory we were able to establish. Thank you for trusting me enough to gain access to you and for giving me an opportunity to care for you and support you. I will forever love you!

I am thankful for my second father, Clinton Bradford, who supported and cared for me as his own daughter for over thirty years.

Although we had some bumps in the road, you still managed to find the paved way. Thank you for teaching me how to follow my dreams and goals in life. I thank God for allowing you to fill in the gap during a crucial time in our lives. Oftentimes, many step/second parents do not take on the tasks or responsibilities to care for children who are not their own. However, you took another approach as a real man/father to provide for me. We've had some tough interactions for many years, but it does not negate the sacrifices you made. You taught me a valuable lesson: hurt people can forgive others. We have overcome many challenges and differences but, yet, respect each other's perspective. Love you and thank you!

I am grateful for my grandparents because they instilled such greatness inside me. To my grandmothers—Rose Carol, Delores Patricia, and Fannie Mae—and my grandfather, Joseph Phillip, Grandparents are truly gifts from God.

- ❖ Rose Carol (may you rest in Peace), you taught me how to read the Bible and the importance of understanding God's Word. You showed me how to fight through obstacles no matter what it seemed like in the moment, and you imparted in me the significance of education. I know you would be very proud of me. Mom-Mom, because of you, I know I am able to withstand many challenges since I watched you overcome many illnesses and trials. I miss you and I love you—Thank you!

❖ Delores Patricia (may you rest in Peace), you inspired me to have faith and to believe in the FATHER'S plan for my life. You displayed such joy and strength no matter what you experienced, and you told me to never give up on my dreams. I know you were very pleased with me and all of my successes. Nanna, because of you, I know that if I put my faith in God, I can do anything. I miss you and I love you— Thank you!

❖ Fannie Mae, you motivated me to have a prayer life and to put everything in God's hands. You encouraged me to hold on and never give up and challenged me in an area that I had no idea I was capable of handling. I know you are joyful for the many goals I have achieved. Grand mom, because of you, I know how to pray because I listened and watched you pray until change happened. I love you—Thank you!

❖ Phillip, you are dear to me and no one can ever change that. Just your humor (which I know I get mine from you) uplifts my spirits. You have always been the same, and I just enjoy talking to you and making you smile. Pop-Pop, thank you for always being consistent and never changing. I love you and I appreciate you so much!

I appreciate my pastor, Bishop Evans, who instilled in me such sincerity and strength. I remember going through a difficult time in my life, from April 2018 to February 2020. I kept asking God, "Why do You keep putting me in these situations?" I wanted and needed a break, but, Bishop, you said something so profound in Bible Study on Wednesday, February 5, 2020; it was like you were speaking directly to me. Bishop, you said, "The process is more important to God than the results because He already promises the results." I had to understand that God was trying to teach me to *trust* His process even when it does not seem to go my way. Bishop, I am grateful to have such a wise man of God in my life. Thank you for always praying and encouraging me even when you did not know I needed it. Much love to you!

I thank God for my best friend, Yemi-Yah; you literally helped me pay my bills and sacrificed a lot of your time supporting and assisting me during this journey. If it were not for your honesty and words of strength, I would have lost so many things along this experience. You have been a true, sincere friend for over 11 years. When I met you Yemi, I knew it was going to be something different about our friendship. You really inspired me to have a different perspective on life, outside of church. I remember singing with various groups for a time and attending so many gospel concerts. All I knew was "Church," and that was it. I really was not enthused about going back to school to further my education; however, your words of inspiration changed my perspective. I was content with life and "running for Jesus," not realizing that I was dying on the inside and losing myself. I remember having several conversations with you about religion, my desires to live for Jesus Christ and to support the local gospel artists. Yemi, your response was "Tee, it's okay; you don't have to attend every concert and support the world." When you said, "Tee, it's time to focus on YOU," in that moment, I knew you cared about my life and my well-being; you had a different type of love for me. I instantly re-registered at Community College of Philadelphia. I was so motivated by you, and we would discuss class assignments and challenge each other's perception of situations. We would pray for each daily, which we still do to this day. Because of you, we were able to graduate together with our Master's degrees from Wilmu—Aye! If I have never said it before (which I am sure I have, LOL), I am truly, truly appreciative to have such a blessed and encouraging friend like you. I love you forever!

To Pastor Maurice Bowser, I honestly appreciate you for your words of wisdom, knowledge, and strength. You have a way of bringing light to a dark situation. You provide so much clarity from a Spiritual stance. I thank God for allowing you to play a major role in my life and to speak truth and certainty. I remember you once said, "Expectation minus observation leads us to frustration. We like to hold on to things we do not want to let go of; so therefore, God will put 'Pressure' on us and cause life to move or stop us." May

God continue to bless you because you are tremendously gifted and anointed. Love you to life!

To my biological siblings—Robert, Shalika, Maalika, Stephanie, Darlene, Cadira, and Tabitha—I love each of you and am forever grateful to have you as my siblings. Although we fight, disagree, and have our differences regarding each other daily, I am still blessed to have each of you in my life. Please know that no matter what hindrances or barriers try to destroy our kinship, I will always fight for our connection.

To my nieces and nephews—Honesty, Mark, Imani, Jai'el, Bradly, Destin. Jada, Nora, JoJo, Nolene....and those unborn (lol)— Aunt Tori will always have your back and will always support you in your successes. Keep inspiring to make a difference in life. Remember to never give up when life seems overpowering. Know you are overcomers and uniquely different. I love you! Stay focused, cut out the unnecessary noise, and be strong!

To my Godparents—Janet Henson, Bishop Joel Adams, and Dee (RIP) and Ashton Smith—thank you for praying for me and constantly instilling in me the importance of having a relationship with God at a young age. I appreciate each of you for impacting my life, not only spiritually but naturally. Your ongoing support never goes unnoticed, and I am appreciative to have such wonderful Godparents. I love you all.

To my Godchildren—Dane, Denim, King, and Delajah—I promise to cover each of you in prayers daily. My goal is to ensure that you receive spiritual, physical, and emotional support from me as needed. I will make sure that I am involved and a blessing to you as much as I can—Proverbs 22:6: *Train up a child in the way he should go; when he is old, he will not depart from it.* I am appreciative to God for allowing me to have the opportunity to be a part of your journeys.

To my close family and friends—Aunt Colleen, Uncle Darren, Uncle Melvin, Justin, Ja'Nea (Fav G-Sis), Ivory & Rickey, Ezra-James, Ervin, Rodney, Momma Pearl (Shawn), Da'Monique, Joya, Torrey Marcel, Sasha, Toya W., Hassan, Kola, Jason, Aunt Tiya, Auntie (Diane Denise), Aunt Joy & Uncle Hicks, LaThina, Rickey, Grand-mom Betty, Grand-mom Lula, Pastor Nick Smith, Aunt Lori, and Lisa Stafford—words cannot express how much I adore and value each of you. I will never ever take for granted the love and support, prayers, encouragement, and authenticity that each of you has demonstrated to me. Thank you so much. I love each and every one of you to Life! A great "Thank You" also goes to my cousins, aunts, uncles, and other church family—the Gees, Barnes, Buchanans, Hectors, Hacketts, Taggarts, Sharps, Gores, Adams, and Joneses; I love you all!

Please contact Art & Legacy Publications for your publishing needs:

artandlegacypublications.com

Made in the USA
Monee, IL
08 August 2021